Creative Crafts for Kids

Arts and CRAFTS
for Myths and Tales

By Greta Speechley

Gareth Stevens
Publishing

Please visit our Web site www.garethstevens.com. For a free color catalog of all our high-quality books, call toll free 1-800-542-2595 or fax 1-877-542-2596.

Library of Congress Cataloging-in-Publication Data
Speechley, Greta, 1948-
 Arts and crafts for myths and tales / Greta Speechley.
  p. cm. — (Creative crafts for kids)
 Includes index.
 ISBN 978-1-4339-3567-1 (library binding)
 ISBN 978-1-4339-3568-8 (pbk.)
 ISBN 978-1-4339-3569-5 (6-pack)
 1. Handicraft—Juvenile literature. I. Title.
TT157.S653 2010
745.5—dc22   2009041573

Published in 2010 by
Gareth Stevens Publishing
111 East 14th Street, Suite 349
New York, NY 10003

© 2010 The Brown Reference Group Ltd.

For Gareth Stevens Publishing:
Art Direction: Haley Harasymiw
Editorial Direction: Kerri O'Donnell

For The Brown Reference Group Ltd:
Editorial Director: Lindsey Lowe
Managing Editor: Tim Harris
Children's Publisher: Anne O'Daly
Design Manager: David Poole
Production Director: Alastair Gourlay

Picture Credits:
All photographs: Martin Norris
Front Cover: Shutterstock: Lunetskaya and Martin Norris

Manufactured in the United States of America
1 2 3 4 5 6 7 8 9   12 11 10   0101

CPSIA compliance information: Batch #BRW0102GS: For further information contact Gareth Stevens, New York, New York at 1-800-542-2595.

Contents

Introduction

Myths are exciting stories with fantastical creatures and characters. Every country has a wealth of tales for you to learn about, and this book is full of projects inspired by some of the most magical stories. There is a Trojan horse toy box from an old Greek myth, and there are mischievous pixies and flitting fairies to make.

YOU WILL NEED

Each project includes a list of all the things you need.

Before you buy new materials, look at home to see what you could use instead. For example, you can cut cardboard shapes out of an empty cereal box.

You can buy other items, such as air-drying clay and felt from a craft shop. You can buy silver sand for the sand painting from a garden center. For the flying fairies, you will need to buy pink kitchen scourers from a grocery store.

Getting started

Read the steps for the project first.

Gather together all the items you need.

Cover your work surface with newspaper.

Wear an apron, or change into old clothes.

A message for adults

All the projects in Arts and Crafts for Myths and Tales have been designed for children to make, but occasionally they will need you to help. Some of the projects do require the use of sharp utensils, such as scissors or needles. Please read the instructions before your child starts work.

Making patterns

Follow these steps to make the patterns on pages 30 and 31. Using a pencil, trace the pattern onto tracing paper. If you're making a project out of fabric, you can cut out the tracing paper pattern and pin it onto the fabric. To cut the pattern out of cardboard, turn the tracing over, and lay it onto the cardboard. Rub firmly over the pattern with a pencil. The shape will appear on the cardboard. Cut out the shape.

When you have finished

Wash paintbrushes, and put everything away.

Put pens, pencils, paints, and glue in an old box or ice-cream container.

Keep scissors and any other sharp items in a safe place.

Stick needles and pins into a pincushion or a piece of scrap cloth.

BE SAFE

Look out for the safety boxes. They will appear whenever you need to ask an adult for help.

Ask an adult to help you use sharp scissors.

Magic amulet

In many tales, the hero or heroine has a magic amulet with special powers. Make your own amulet, and see if it brings you good luck.

YOU WILL NEED

white plastic drink bottle	purple foil candy wrappers
marker pen	silver spray paint
scissors	
gold and purple thin tinsel	hole punch
	black cord
small, round candle base	plastic bag tie
	needle
shiny purple bobble	glue

1 Mark off a section on the plastic drink bottle that is about 3in (7.5cm) tall and goes about halfway around the bottle. Cut it out.

2 Punch holes along the sides of the armband using a hole punch, and make two holes at either end. Spray the band silver.

6

3 Thread thin gold tinsel along the edges. Make two holes in the candle base and in the middle of the armband using a needle. Push a plastic bag tie through both pieces, and twist the ends.

4 Glue purple tinsel onto the amulet around the candle case. Wind some more gold tinsel into a tight coil, and glue the coil inside the candle holder.

5 Glue a shiny purple bobble to the center. Scrunch purple foil wrappers into balls, and glue them on either side of the centerpiece. Thread two black cords through the holes in the amulet so you can tie it around your arm.

Snake demon

This fierce snake demon from Sri Lanka is said to frighten away evil spirits. The hissing snakes are made from twisted newspaper covered with papier-mâché.

YOU WILL NEED

newspaper	tissue paper
cardboard	PVA glue
scissors	mixing bowl
pencil	poster paints
tape	paintbrush

1 Draw the demon's face onto cardboard. Draw three wiggly snakes at the top for hair and two large nostrils in the middle. Cut out the demon drawing.

8

2 Cut two snake heads out of cardboard, and tape them to the face so they are coming out of the nostrils! Tape on a forked tongue at the bottom, too. Twist pieces of newspaper, and tape them over the lines you have drawn for the snake hair and the nostrils. Tape on balls of newspaper for eyes.

3 To make a nose, cut a piece of cardboard that fits around the nostrils. Tape it in place.

4 Mix up half PVA glue and half water in a mixing bowl. Tear up strips of tissue paper, and paste them all over the snake demon. Let each layer dry, and paste on three layers in total.

5 Have fun painting your snake demon, and then hang it up on your door to keep out pests!

Little lyre

One Greek myth tells how the god Hermes invented the lyre. He scooped out a tortoise and used the shell as a musical instrument to charm the other gods. Make a lyre from paper plates, and charm everyone by singing along as you strum!

YOU WILL NEED

four paper plates	tape
pencil	short piece of bamboo or dowel
scissors	
felt-tip pens	small plastic beads
wooden skewer	scissors
black wool	glue

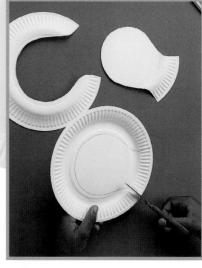

1 Cut two horseshoe shapes out of two paper plates. They make the arms of the lyre.

2 Cut a curved piece out of a third paper plate. Do this by drawing around the edge of one of the arm pieces. It makes one side of the body of the lyre.

10

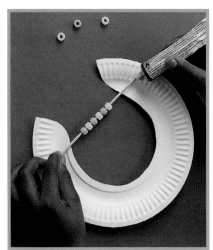

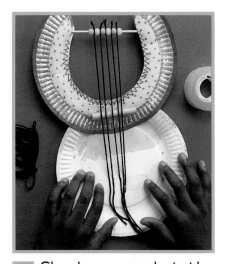

3 Color in the pieces. Take a fourth plate, and decorate it in a tortoiseshell pattern. This will be the other side of the body of the lyre.

4 Thread six beads onto a wooden skewer. Glue the skewer to the back of one of the arm pieces. Glue the second arm piece on top.

5 Glue the arms to the inside of the tortoiseshell piece. Color in the inside as shown because this part will show. Glue a short piece of bamboo or dowel to the bottom of the arms for the strings to rest on. To make the strings, tie lengths of wool between the beads, and tape them in place farther down.

6 Glue the last piece over the strings as shown.

11

Sand painting

The Navajo people from the Southwest are famous for making spectacular sand paintings on the ground. In Navajo healing ceremonies, a sick person sits on the sand picture, and then the sand is rubbed over his or her body.

YOU WILL NEED

silver sand (sandpit sand)	white cardboard
mixing bowl	glue
mixing stick	paintbrush
poster paints	wooden picture frame
pestle and mortar or a stone	scissors
pencil	cord
scrap cardboard	

1 Mix up sand with a little paint. Spread out the sand on cardboard to dry. Crush any lumps in the sand with a stone. You could use a pestle and mortar to grind the sand smooth if you have one. Make four or five colors of sand.

2 Cut out a rectangle of white cardboard to fit in your wooden frame. Draw on a design using a pencil.

3 Paint glue onto the area you want to color, then sprinkle on colored sand. To make the rocket picture on the opposite page, we sprinkled on glitter as well.

4 Shake off the extra sand, and glue another area. Sprinkle on a different color of sand.

5 Let the glue dry, and then fit the picture into a wooden frame. Put the back on the frame. Press down the tabs on the back of the frame to keep the picture in place.

13

Glinting dagger

Every hero or heroine needs a weapon to help them fight off mythical beasts. Decorate this dagger with a glittering hilt (handle), then make up an adventurous myth starring you as the brave hero.

YOU WILL NEED

strong cardboard	scissors
tracing paper	glitter pens in different colors
pencil	
ruler	kitchen foil
glue	

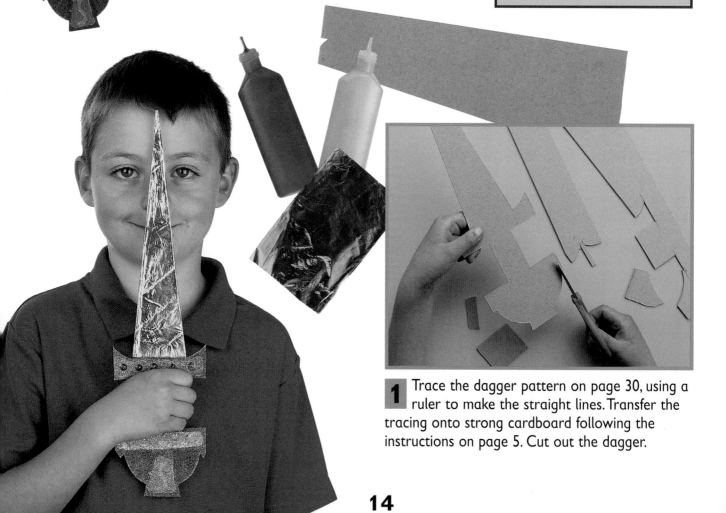

1 Trace the dagger pattern on page 30, using a ruler to make the straight lines. Transfer the tracing onto strong cardboard following the instructions on page 5. Cut out the dagger.

2 Cover the blade with kitchen foil, and stick it down with glue. Smooth the foil surface with your thumbs to get rid of wrinkles.

3 Decorate the hilt with glitter pens. We have drawn on an outline with green glitter and added a fan pattern with purple glitter.

4 Fill in the pattern and the background using different-colored glitter pens. Let one side dry thoroughly before decorating the other.

15

Pixie pen tops

Pixies are tiny characters from English folk stories. They love playing tricks such as pointing travelers in the wrong direction and blowing out candles!

YOU WILL NEED

air-drying clay
pencil
poster paints
thin paintbrush
varnish
clay cutter

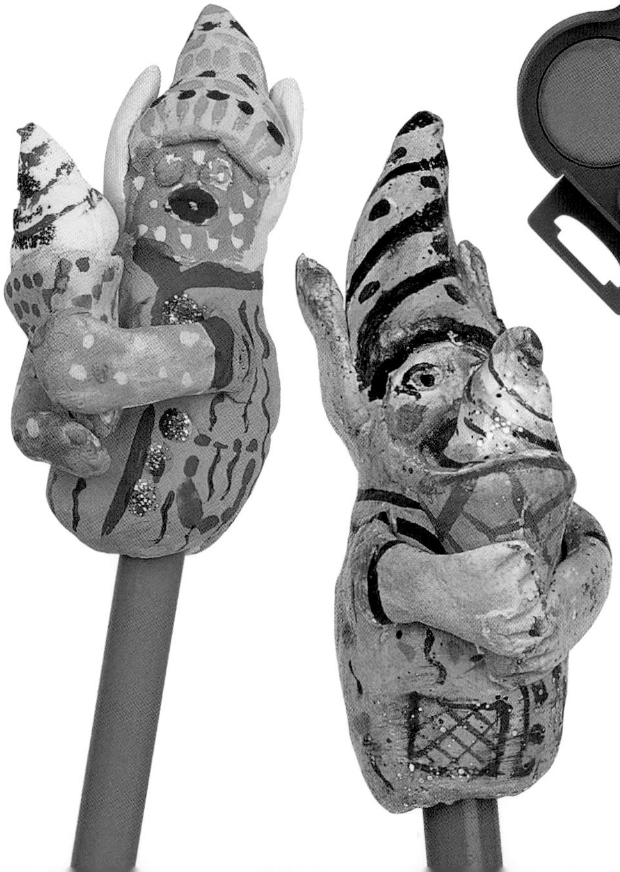

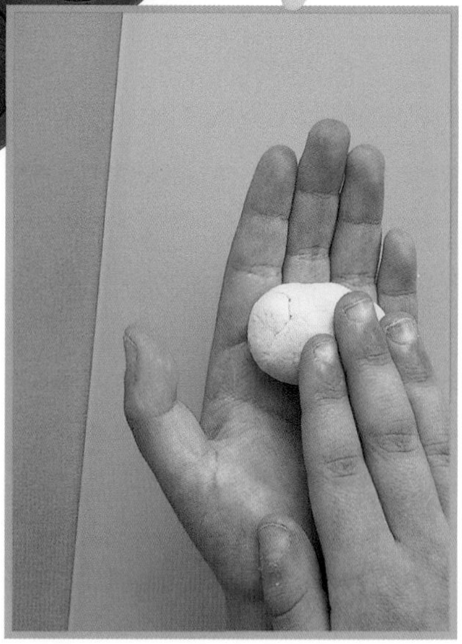

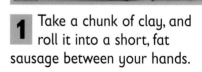

1 Take a chunk of clay, and roll it into a short, fat sausage between your hands.

16

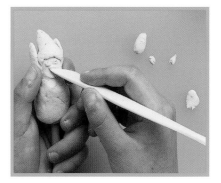

2 Push the end of a pencil securely into the end of the chunk of clay.

3 Shape the clay into a body with a head by squeezing it with your fingers.

4 Make a pointy pixie hat and pointy ears from clay. Press them onto the pixie's head. Press on tiny balls of clay for eyes, a nose, and a mouth.

5 Our pixie has stolen an ice cream! Make an ice-cream cone from clay, and roll two sausages for arms. Press them onto the pixie, with the arms folding around the cone. You can use a modeling tool such as a clay cutter to add detail to your pixie's clothes.

6 Take the pixie off the pencil, and let the clay dry and harden. Paint the pixie and his ice cream with lots of bright colors. You will need a very thin paintbrush. Let the paint dry. Paint the pixie with a layer of varnish to give it a shiny finish.

17

Pot of gold

Have you heard the tale that at the end of every rainbow there is a pot of gold? This is a charming golden money box with a rainbow chute to slide your coins down.

YOU WILL NEED

thin cardboard	gold paper
tracing paper	glue
pencil	felt in different colors
scissors	poster paints
round yogurt container	paintbrush
box	paper

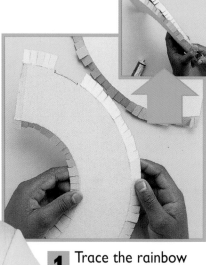

1 Trace the rainbow pattern on page 31. Transfer the shape onto thin cardboard following the instructions on page 5. Do this twice, and cut out the two shapes. Glue the pieces together using the tabs. The coin slots must line up together.

2 Paint a rainbow onto white paper using a watery brush. Make it slightly bigger than the cardboard rainbow. Glue it onto the cardboard rainbow chute.

3 Choose a box, and cut a slot in the side of it for the rainbow to fit into. Paint a wash of blue onto white cardboard to make a sky background. Glue it to the back of the box. Glue the rainbow chute to the sky with its end over the slot in the box.

4 Cut the bottom out of a yogurt container, and cut out a section from the side. This is the pot of gold. Cover it in gold paper, and fit it around the bottom of the rainbow. Glue it in place.

5 Cover the box with green felt. Make a spiky fringe at the top to look like grass. Cut out felt flowers, and glue them on. Glue a white paper cloud to the sky, too.

Phoenix clip

The ancient Egyptians told stories about a fabulous bird called the phoenix. They said it had scarlet and gold feathers and lived for about 500 years! Add a clip and a magnet to your phoenix so it can hold notes and lists in its beak.

YOU WILL NEED

tracing paper	gold and silver glitter pens
pencil	glue
gold paper	magnet
felt in different colors	clothes clip
six flexible straws	feathers from a clothes store
tape	scissors
cardboard	

1 Trace the phoenix on page 31. Transfer the tracing onto cardboard, following the instructions on page 5. Cut out the shape. Trace the phoenix again onto a separate piece of cardboard. This time, cut out the beak, head, and leg shapes separately. Use the pieces as templates to cut out a beak from gold paper, a red felt body, a pink felt head, and blue felt legs. Cut the felt slightly bigger than the templates.

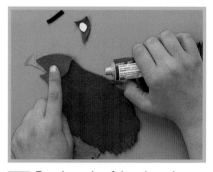

2 Feather the felt edges by making small snips with the scissors. Glue the pieces onto the cardboard bird. Cut out an eye from purple felt and a white felt iris and black pupil. Glue them on.

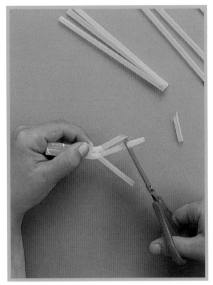

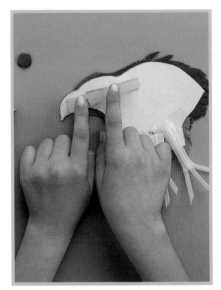

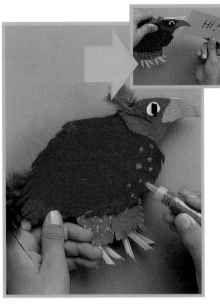

3 To make a foot, tape three flexible straws together just above the bend. Cut them to size, and cut the feet at an angle to make pointy claws. Make a second foot, and tape them to the back of the bird's legs.

4 Glue a clothes clip to the back of the bird, with the clamping end near the beak. Glue a magnet to the clip.

5 Decorate the bird with dots of glitter. Glue feathers to the tail and the top of the head. Your phoenix can hold a note in its beak. You can attach it to the door of the fridge.

Cyclops eye

A cyclops is a giant with one eye in the middle of his forehead. In Greek myths, the cyclops giants make thunderbolts for the god Zeus, and the giants also gobble up people!

Ask an adult to read step 1 and make the paper pulp.

YOU WILL NEED

small egg crate	jar lid
saucepan	clay cutter
food processor	poster paints
stirring spoon	paintbrush
bowl	clear glue
PVA glue	brooch back

1 Tear up the egg crate into pieces, and put them in a bowl. Cover them with water, and let them soak for a couple of days. Ask an adult to boil the mixture in a saucepan for about 20 minutes and then smash it up into a pulp in a food processor. Pour the pulp into a sieve, and squeeze out most of the water.

2 Put the pulp into a bowl, and add a big blob of PVA glue. Stir up the mixture to make a sticky pulp.

3 Use a clay cutter to press a layer of pulp into the jar lid.

4 To make the pupil, roll up a ball of pulp, and press it on. Shape an eyelid from more of the pulp, and press it onto the rim of the jar lid. Let the eye dry thoroughly.

5 Paint the pulp eye in gruesome colors. Let the paint dry.

6 Glue a brooch pin to the back of the jar lid so you can wear the eye as a badge.

Totem pole

In the Northwest, the Tlingit people carve logs to make totem poles. The characters on a totem pole are often animals and mythical creatures. Make your own totem pole with unusual animal faces.

Ask an adult to check that the tin cans have no sharp edges

1 Tape the empty tin cans together to make the totem pole. Be careful in case the cans have sharp edges. Ask an adult to check for you.

YOU WILL NEED

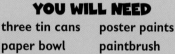

three tin cans	poster paints
paper bowl	paintbrush
cardboard	tissue paper
tape	PVA glue
scissors	mixing bowl
glue	egg crate

2 Cut the paper bowl in half, and glue the two pieces together to make the head crest. Cut up an egg crate to make noses and beaks for your characters.

24

3 Tape the head crest to the top of the pole.

4 Tape on the egg-crate beaks, and cut out two wings from cardboard. Tape them to the sides of the totem pole. Scrunch up tissue paper into balls, and tape them to the pole to make eyes for the creatures.

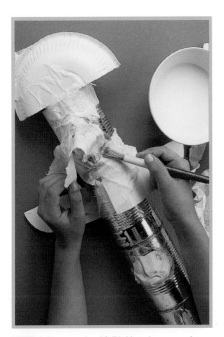

5 Mix up half PVA glue and half water in a bowl. Tear up strips of tissue paper, and paste them all over the totem pole. Let each layer dry, and paste on two or three layers in all.

6 Paint the totem pole in bright colors, one animal on top of another.

Trojan horse

A famous legend tells how the Greeks gave a huge wooden horse as a gift to the city of Troy. When the people of Troy were asleep, Greek soldiers leaped out of the horse and overtook the city! Make a horse of your own as a toy box.

1 To make the legs, cut a fringe of tabs around the top and bottom of four bathroom tissue tubes. Bend back the tabs. Cover the legs with orange felt.

YOU WILL NEED

large box for the body	four bathroom tissue tubes
small juice carton for the head	cork
	scissors
orange, black, and white felt	strong cardboard for the base
scissors	two wooden skewers
pen	
glue	

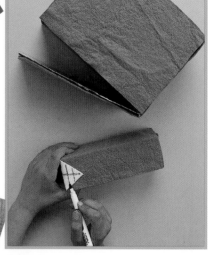

2 Cover the box and the juice carton with orange felt to make the horse's head and body. Make a lift-up lid for the body by cutting along three sides at the top, but leaving one side in place. Glue onto the head a mouth cut from white felt. Draw on teeth with a pen.

26

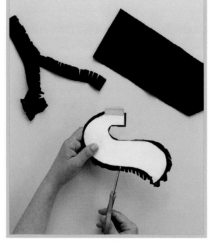

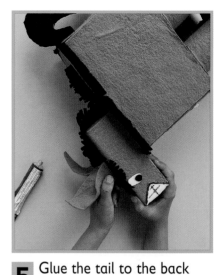

3 Glue the legs to the bottom of the body using the tabs. Glue the head to the lid flap on the top of the body.

4 Trace the tail shape on page 30. Transfer the tracing onto cardboard following the instructions on page 5. Cut out the cardboard tail. Cut two pieces of black felt slightly bigger than the tail. Do this by drawing around the cardboard. Glue them to either side of the tail, and cut a fringe around the edge.

5 Glue the tail to the back of the body using the tab. Cut a fringe of black felt to go around the horse's body and head. Cut out ears from orange felt and eyes from white and black felt. Glue them to the horse's head.

6 To make the base, tape two skewers to a piece of strong cardboard. Push slices of cork onto the ends of the skewers to make wheels. Ask an adult to cut the cork for you. Now glue the horse on top using the tabs on the legs.

Ask an adult to cut a cork to make the wheels.

Flying fairies

Fairies are tiny magical creatures that appear in stories all over the world. They are pretty and charming, and these have lovely pink skirts made from kitchen scourers! Make a few fairies to hang from a flowery mobile in your bedroom.

YOU WILL NEED

round, pink kitchen scourer

four wooden beads for heads

multicolored wool for hair

golden wire for the bodies

small beads for hands and feet

thread

dried moss

green tinsel

fabric flowers

butterfly hair clips

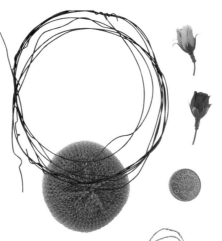

1 To make the first fairy, cut a snip in the center of a kitchen scourer. Cut off a layer of scourer to make a fairy skirt.

2 Bend a piece of golden wire in half to make two long legs, and push it through the center of the skirt. Wind more golden wire around the middle to keep the skirt and legs in place. Leave two ends sticking out to be the arms.

28

3 Thread beads onto the ends of the legs and arms to make feet and hands. Thread a big wooden bead onto the loop of wire at the top to make the fairy's head.

4 Push multicolored wool through the loop sticking out at the top of the bead head. This is fairy hair. Shape golden wire into two fairy wings, and wind them around the fairy's body. Make three fairies in this way.

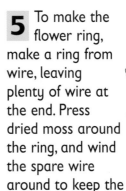

5 To make the flower ring, make a ring from wire, leaving plenty of wire at the end. Press dried moss around the ring, and wind the spare wire around to keep the moss in place. Wind green tinsel around the ring, and push in fabric flowers. Add butterfly hair clips, too. Wind on three more lengths of wire so you can hang up the mobile. Tie the fairies to the ring with thin thread.

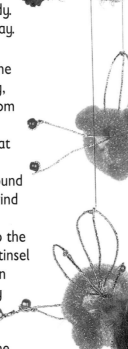

Patterns

Here are the patterns you will need to make some of the projects. To find out how to make a pattern, follow the instructions in the "Making patterns" box on page 5. Sometimes you will need to cut out two shapes using the same tracing. This is indicated on the pattern.

Glinting dagger
page 14

Trojan horse
page 26

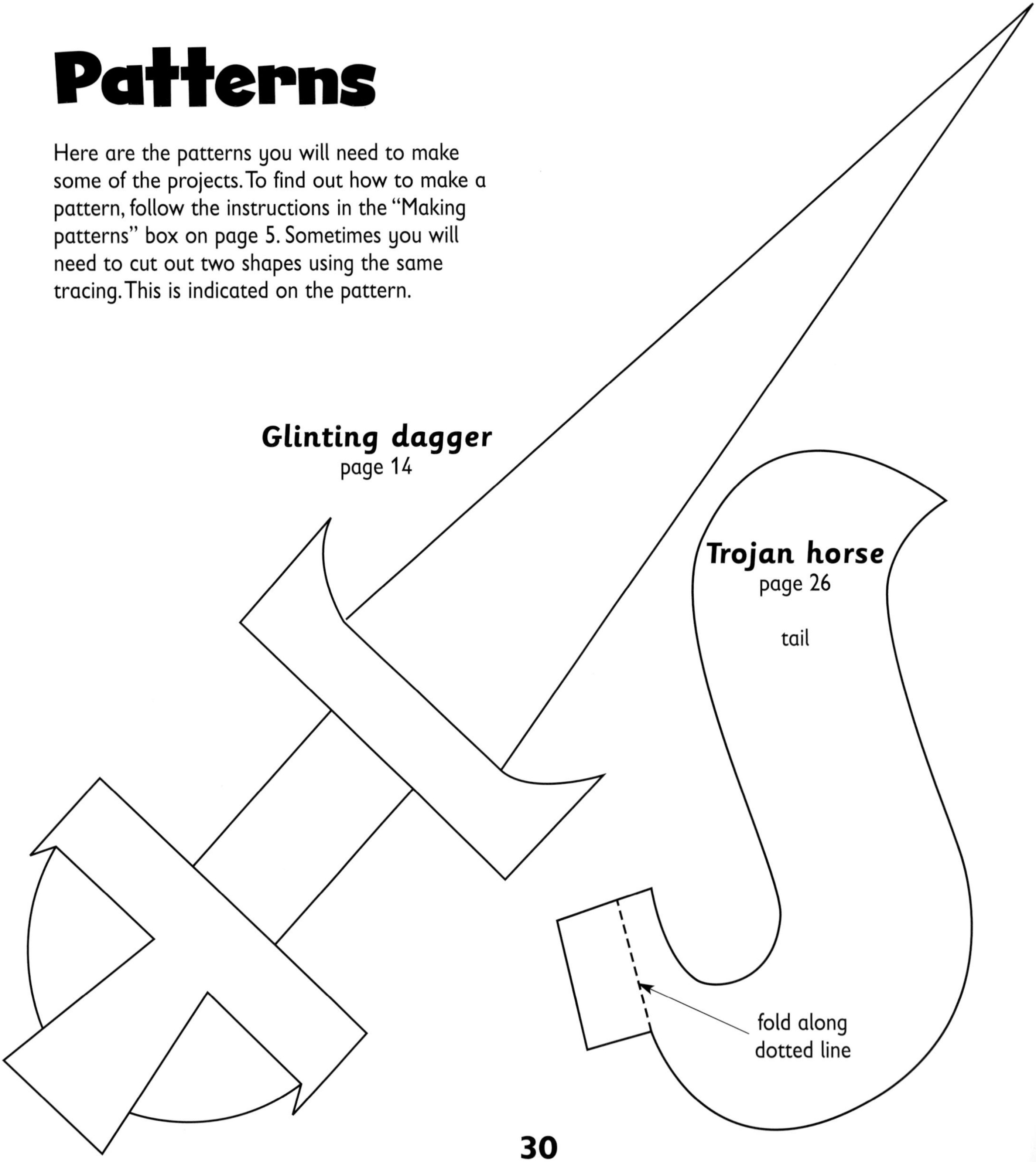

tail

fold along
dotted line

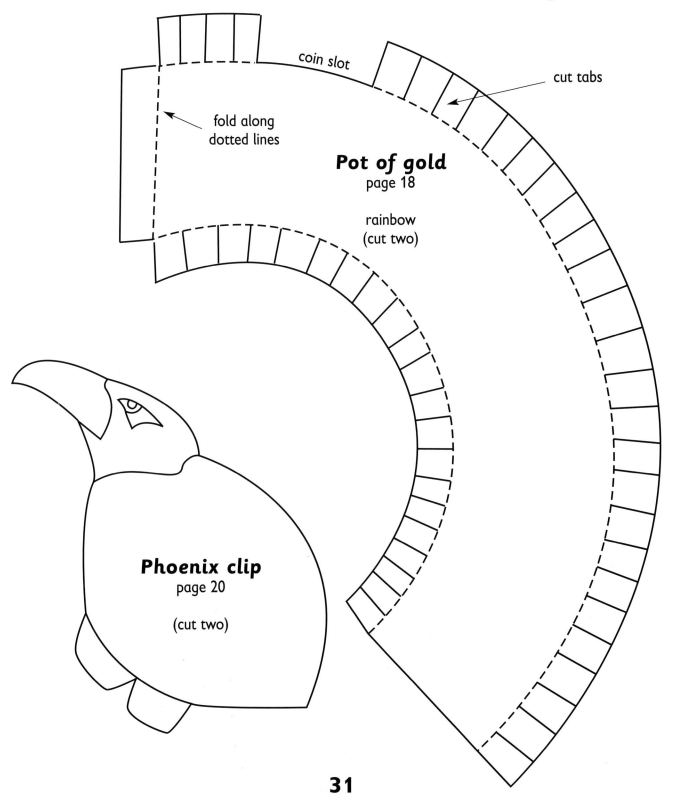

coin slot

cut tabs

fold along
dotted lines

Pot of gold
page 18

rainbow
(cut two)

Phoenix clip
page 20

(cut two)

Glossary

amulet a piece of jewelry that protects against evil, injury, or bad luck

bobble a small object used as decoration

dowel a short wooden peg used to join two pieces of wood

flitting moving quickly from one place to another

fringe a decorative border consisting of short strands of thread or other material

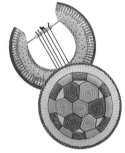

lyre a plucked string instrument with a U-shaped frame

mortar a heavy bowl in which substances are ground into pieces or powder

pestle an object with a round end used for crushing or grinding

PVA glue one of the most common glues. "PVA" stands for polyvinyl acetate.

scourer a scrubbing pad used to clean pots and pans

skewer a thin metal or wooden rod with a pointed end

tinsel a thin strip of glittering foil, paper, or plastic used for decoration

Trojan relating to the ancient city of Troy in what is today Turkey

varnish a substance that gives an object a protective gloss, or the act of applying this substance

Index